Dear Entrepreneur

A Small Business Diary

CITERRA ROBINSON

BookLeaf Publishing

India | USA | UK

Presentation by *BookLeaf Publishing*

Web: www.bookleafpub.com

E-mail: info@bookleafpub.com

ISBN: 9789357443937

First edition 2022

ACKNOWLEDGEMENT

I would like to acknowledge my father for giving me the nickname "SUCCESSFUL". A name that I never aspired to live up to, but indirectly impacted every choice that I have ever made in life. My father had a long generation of God believers in his family—which at a very young age was passed down to me.

Therefore, my faith in Christ was the main drive and sources of hope to accomplish things in this life that I never imagined. I would like to thank my dear aunt Elaine, for her continued inspiration that catapulted me into realm of entrepreneurship; without her charismatic enthusiasm—I would have never truly stepped out on faith. To my brothers, I appreciate the fact that you told me never to allow the opinions of others stand in my way. Thank you for allowing me to be myself. To my sister Ashley; you are a light for me. While many believed in who I could become—your words of encouragement touched my heart in a very different way. And to a host of others who imparted so much into my life. Their love and encouragement throughout this journey was truly vital.

Truthfully, I would not be able to get anything done without the support of my accountability partner and friend K. Chisem. To my lovely husband, my soulmate, best friend and love of my life; Shunpaul Robinson– for his unwavering love and support of my dreams. My children: Gavin, Shunpaul Jr., and Lauryn are my worlds and inspire me to be a better version of myself day to day. Lastly, my Readers, never negotiate your purpose and positioning in this life. Go for what you are good at… master that art; the world will remember you for it.

TABLE OF CONTENTS

A Prayer for All Small Businesses

Dear God, Our Father, and Creator.
I ask today that You bless every small business.
Lord, let Your favor rain down upon them.
And make what was once small—
Larger than anyone can imagine.
Thank you for allowing us to begin this journey
to our purpose–
and doing what we were created to do.
Father hide us from any snare of the enemy.
Because your word
—tells us that 'no weapon formed against us
shall prosper'.
Thank you for the open doors.
And the ones that closed.
We know that Your timing is divine.
And trusting You means trusting the process.
Forgive us oh God if we lost hope.
and succumb to the growing pains.
For this too shall pass.

Amen.

What If?

What if? I am not good enough.
What if? Things don't go as planned.
What if? The service that I provide…
Does not fulfill the consumer's demand.

What if? What I am doing has already been
done.
What if? What sets me apart from others—really
isn't a NEW idea at all.
What if? This is too big of a risk.
What if? I don't see success.
What If? The things that I'm doing—doesn't
make me stand out from the rest.

What if? I get shamed on social media
For one simple mistake.
What if? My name is smeared and my company
tanks.
Surely, I couldn't rise from the ridicule and
shame.
And to think I've invested so much to build this.

What if? The bad reviews outweigh the good
ones.
What if? Life happens and I have to take a
break.

What if? I fail…

What if they say… 'I am dreaming too big.
And that 'I should get my head out of the
clouds'.
What if their opinion of me just doesn't fall to
the ground?

I'm so tired of living in the state of 'WHAT IF?'
You can take that saying right to the grave.
Hear lies the expectation of negative thinking—
Here lies the deception of their belief..
Because
What if my company… changes the GAME!

Many Are the Plans

Okay.
I think I got it figured out.
My next move– that is…
Yet something in the back of my mind tells me
—my plans aren't in alignment with His.

Therefore, I PRAY and I FAST.
RENEW… then repeat.
To ensure it's His voice I'm hearing
—so, this journey doesn't end in defeat.

I tread lightly the path—not to step out of God's
will.
Aware of the obstacle that may lie ahead.
…Fear
…Doubt
…Insecurities
Are all the emotions that try to contend.
But I remember that 'faith without work is
dead'.

So, I press myself forward trying to prepare for
the unprepared.
With faith being the belief in the unforeseen
I continue to walk UNAFRAID.

Because we can plan all we want.
—yet still not reach the mark.
My Purpose was predestined in HIM.
Therefore, I trust in the One who judges the
heart.

Many are the plans that man can make.
However, human judgment is bound to error.
I much rather counsel a benevolent power.
Because it's law!
HIS purpose will prevails
—and supersede our endeavors.

Doubt

6

When I feel it…I wish I never felt it.
When I say it… I wish I never spoke it.
When I think it… I wish I never thought it.
Then when I look back on it—
I smile at where I am now; then laugh about it.

Because doubt is only a moment of thinking.
It never lasts.
And it will not hold any weight on ones
perception as a whole.

Always look forward.
Learn from what is behind you.
Trust God's plan and keep moving forward.

You will reach success in the end.

Post Doubt

I said something I shouldn't have.
My words will eventually be returned.

My actions have brought on much conviction.
My lessons have been learned.

This journey is becoming much easier.
My joy is starting to come.

The doubt I once gave meaning.
Did not shape what my business has become.

Not My Reality

They say that FEAR is nothing but a
Fragment of 'false evidence appearing real'.
Yet in this moment this fragment of reality is all
I can see.
And every emotion that I am feeling
—is only getting more real to me.

They say the word 'NO' simply means
—waiting for the NEXT OPPORTUNITY..
And that you grow the most from the NO's.
But I feel…
if I get rejected one more time my true emotions
are going to show.

The Bible says
'But the race is not given to the swift'.
Therefore, I avoid picking up the pace.
Meanwhile seeing others getting much further in
the race.

Am I not managing my time?
Am I moving too slow?
Am I not pouring enough into my journey?
Therefore, I don't see growth.

Nevertheless, I'll keep hope alive.
and have joy in all I do.
I'm sure my endurance will be rewarded if I just
keep going
—remain steadfast and push through.

Un-PRODUCTIVE

Coffee… just doesn't work anymore.
I don't want to get out of bed.
I don't want to set goals.
I am not myself.
Who is this person? Where did I go?
How many failed attempts will it take to
succeed?
I might not ever know.
But I feel like it's all me…
Just being engulfed in what things looks like
right now.
—caught up my feelings and really just numb.
It's funny I can envision myself outside of this
phase.
Where life is simple and way more fun.

Yet my current life is being placed on a stage.
And I honestly cannot get past Act One.

One day…
I've had ENOUGH.
I want to truly give up.
I wish I had a towel I could throw in.
Preferably WHITE.

But this one is soaked in tears, sweat, and mucus
all from last night.

Next Day…
I can do this.
Pain only endures for a night.
And this moment will not take me out.
Yeah, bet!

Nevertheless, through a 24hr. day they all are
seemingly looking identical.
And my up days and are feeling like down days.
And my down days are looking like up days.
But it is only Tuesday.

However, I understand my frustration doesn't
stem from these feelings.
I don't like feeling this way at all..
And would much rather focus on healing—
to prevent me from constantly hitting this brick
wall.

I want to drink coffee… because I enjoy it.
I want to sit at the end of my bed in the morning
and stretch from a good night's rest.
I want to look back on the goal I set and think…
YES! to myself.
I want to go back to being me.
When I was productive.

Happy and goal oriented.
Filled with drive and motivation.

Shake it off…
I will get there… just press through and trust the
process and pressure.
I will only be better for it.

Distracted

How set are you on accomplishing your goals?
How well do you manage your time?
Is discipline your struggle as a whole?
Or do tasks just cross your mind.
Entrepreneurship is not for all.
Most definitely not the faint of heart.
When you are in a state of being
overwhelmed—
Are you liable to fall apart?
How well do you deal with being distracted?
Can you push pass and be proactive?
Or is life all too much?
Just know whatever can go wrong will go
wrong.
You just have to overcome.
If all things just came smooth and easy to you.
Nothing would be appreciated.
Because victory doesn't taste as good if you
don't get a little frustrated.

Just ask the wealthiest people around.

Just When…

Just when…
Things appear to be falling in line and going
well.
Something, just something, seems to go wrong.
But this, remember, is only a phase—
and shall not last too long.

Small Business… Bright Future

People love to put you in their box of
expectation.
Yet envy you for marching to the beat of your
own drum.
They want to see you rise to every occasion.
Yet don't understand when you need to be alone.
So take your time.
Block out the chatter.
Move at your own pace.
in the end—
when doors open and close.
Those same people will be in your face.

Your Brand

To protect your name…
You have to be willing to do whatever it takes.
By fixing your wrongs.
And rectifying your mistakes.
By offering a refund if your contract isn't tight.
By knowing for sure that the customer is always
right (in some cases).
Giving your best service.
No matter the situation.
By answering frequently asked questions
without hesitation.
By making sure your service is truly guaranteed.
By completing a task at a reasonable speed.
By greeting all with a smile.
And pleasant salutations.
By being clear with your goals and meeting
expectations.

Dear Entrepreneur

I see you over there.
Wondering what comes next.
Yet have seen what you've done.

What little work you thought you've put in
—has gotten you several steps past
square one.

You have so much to be proud of right now.
But please don't brag or boast.
Because your time is what you sacrificed
and that's what counts the most.

Therefore, be glad entrepreneur
you still have quite some road ahead.
But it's better to have a positive direction
— than to constantly be misled.

Remain Humble

Humility is vital
—as your business begins to grow.
Therefore, beware of a pending ego.

Remember it is hard to speak words of wisdom
to those who are in need.
When as a caveat
—they constantly hear the things that you've
achieved.

Thus, I urge you.
Stay fixated on your story.
Because the fruits of your labor
—will reveal your glory.

Still

I'm still standing after all those closed doors.
I still smile behind the tears.
The battle continues after many loss wars.
But I can not be stifled by fear.
I'm persistent in my pursuit to greatness.
Fortified by my drive.
Destined to reach for the sun—
Because I won't be satisfied with just the skys.

Step-By-Step

I think I can.
I think I can.
But isn't it better to know?
That doubt my friend…
—should not be allowed in.
Because it will hinder your growth.

The ups and downs are inevitable.
But don't focus on variables
uncontrolled.
Life itself can be quite messy.
So why carry the unnecessary load.

Henceforth, declare with confidence I add.
I KNOW IN ALL THINGS I CAN…
because if you don't feel that within yourself
your business doesn't stand a chance.

Mind Set

Where do you see your business—
in the next 5 to 7 years?
Now think of the sacrifice that has got to take.
Be sure to leave room for error
And erroneous behavior.
Because perfection succumbs to mistakes.
One might think…
Motivation… Ambition… and Tenacity is
enough.
However, without discipline like many journeys
—the road might be quite tough.
The point I'm trying to make is…
that strong will is the minuscule part.
Because if your mindset doesn't evolve—
where you see yourself in 5 to 7 years.
Is like going through a gallery of abstract art.

Motto

Have you ever heard?
That once a task has begun—
You never leave…until it's done.
No matter the task BIG or small—
Do it right or not at all.

Or…

NO, simply means that the Next Opportunities
will come.

Maybe…

If you never take a risk—
You will work for the one that did.

My dad always said…

That a temper is a good thing to have as long as
you don't lose it.

No matter what keeps you going…
Just keep going!

The Great Unknown

Never be afraid of what you don't know—
how else will you ever find out.
Don't be too to quick for fear to STOP you in
your tracks—
because you'll never encounter doubt.
See doubt only comes when you've been doing
something for a while.
But things stopped going as smoothly as
planned.
Yet how on earth can you go through the
motions—
if you don't try firsthand.
This road will be rocky…
Bumpy and bruised.
But if you remain persistent—
Things are bound to turn out smooth.

Can You See It?

I saw this before in a dream.
That I would be larger than life.
The satisfaction that came with motherhood and
marriage.
Yet I've always known I'd be more than a
mother and a wife.

I saw it before when I was young.
That there was more in life that I was meant to
do.
That purpose was always inside of me.
The lies the world told
—were eventually outgrew.

Nevertheless, this journey was scary.
The path was never clear.
My mind was always so boggled.
And reaching success seemed light years away.

At some point I even got tired.
People telling me not to focus on dismay.
But how can a person not have tunnel vision…
—when EVERYTHING and I do mean
EVERYTHING,
is not going their way.

Had they put themselves in my shoes.
They'd see how hard it was to walk.
It's like my life was a treadmill.
And the journey was never going to stop.

But look at me now.
All cool, calm, and collected…
Things actually went better than
— even I expected.

Proper Planning

26

It would be easier to keep your ducks in a row.
If they did not keep walking out of line.
But I'd future advise.
—you control things…
That ONLY you can.
Because this is not how ducks were designed.

Think about it…

Purpose

This is the moment you were created for.
Do not second guess this time.
The life you've lead up to this point
—only created the space for you to truly shine.
So while you will feel growing pains.
Remember growth is yet occurring.
But if you choose to give in too early…
It's only your purpose you're hurting.